CONTENTS

INTRODUCTION

Over successive legacies, the French have unearthed, amidst their family albums, many an old black and white photograph of a soldier that served in the 1914-18 war. Most often, they are unable to put a name to these unknown faces. Yet, these pictures are the very soul of the conflict. The faces of these soldiers are full of fear, suffering; they evoke broken bodies, life and often death, but they also bear witness to the camaraderie and moments of distraction enjoyed by those we have come to call the Poilus. To breathe life back into these pictures, we must first of all replace them within their historical context. As such, they can offer a genuine journey into the intimacy of the Great War soldiers of France, not only through their experience of the Champagne trenches, of the Verdun hell and of all other fields of combat on the Western Front, but also during their moments of weariness and great solitude, far from their families and their homeland.

1914

The 113rd Infantry Regiment - Blois, led by its offi cers and flag, on its way to its mobilisation station, ready to head for the front.

FROM GENERAL MOBILISATION TO STALEMATE

General mobilisation

The harvest tocsin had sounded three times on the 1st of August 1914 when France's farm workers, busy at their chores, learned with astonishment and emotion that France was mobilising troops. They all delved into their sideboards to unearth their military booklets. Inside each booklet, a mobilisation form indicated which regimental depot each man was to head for. Then, appropriately equipped from head to toe, the ordinary citizen became a soldier. All conversations converged, "War or not?" For, since the assassination of the Archduke Franz Ferdinand of AustriaHungary and of his wife, on the 28th of June 1914 in Sarajevo in Bosnia, far from the French frontiers, an irreversible spiral had begun. The game of allegiances (Triple Alliance: AustriaHungary, Germany and Italy, the Triple Entente: France, Russia and Great Britain) could but lead to war, which was declared by Germany against France on the 3rd of August 1914. Restrained jubilation hit the streets. The newformed regiments left their garrisons to head for railway stations where, according to a formal mobilisation plan, special trains would take them to the front. Wives and children accompanied soldiers. Separation was a painful process, yet their duty towards their fatherland awaited them – a duty to seize back Alsace and Lorraine from German hands. And, after all, had it not been said that this would be a short war?

▲ *War had not yet been declared; however, these GVC soldiers (road and railway guards) from post 10 in Moulins (Allier) were ready to do battle, with an idealistic vision of a war that still seemed so far away.*

▲ *German machine gun with its gunners in firing position.*

▲ *The wagons that had taken the French regiments to the front were later used to evacuate the wounded towards hospitals established to the rear. The patriotic slogans drawn in chalk on these wagons already seem a long way off.*

▼ *August-September 1914. The medical service was overwhelmed by the incessant flow of wounded troops and improvised first aid positions were hastily set up. Note the perceptible anguish on the face of the woman to the left.*

August 1914: the bloody summer

Following the mobilisation scheme referred to as Plan XVII, the armies were already gathered at the borders. On the 4th of August 1914, when Germany violated Belgium's neutrality, French and British troops immediately headed for Belgian territory to offer support. Columns of refugees were the sign of the approaching war. Despite fierce resistance, the Belgian Army pained to counter the German steamroller.

From north to east, the French armies advanced and their grand entrance into liberated Mulhouse caused much ado (8th August 1914).

Then nothing... the "Red Trousers", exhausted by their long marches, were giving way in Belgium. German patrols had been spotted in the Ardennes and throughout liberated Alsace; contact was imminent. But the French soldiers were already under shellfire. Showers of steel from heavy artillery, a field in which Germany was ahead of France who, to retaliate, could only rely on its famous French 75 gun – highly accurate at short range, but totally inefficient for long-distance firing. The enemy was at last in sight, running along the hedges, on the forest edge. Officers gave their orders, "bayonets to guns" and the troops thrust forwards. Opposite, the machine guns sputtered, entire ranks of soldiers fell to the ground – survivors made no protest, returning to their positions which they strove simply to maintain. Although idealised and relatively theoretical, this scene at least demonstrates the extent to which the French Army was ill-prepared for modern warfare: repetitive attack was the prevailing tactic.

1914 1915 1916 1917 1918

Attacks doomed to failure, before an enemy with superior men and equipment, the names of which went down in history: Morhange (20th-23rd August), Charleroi (22nd-23rd August). From north to east, the French armies withdrew.
Concern escalated throughout the villages of France. Parents and wives who had received no news of mobilised troops eagerly read the official communiqué. On the 25th of August 1914, they could barely believe their eyes as they learned that the front was "stable from the Somme to the Vosges". War had struck French soil!
On the front, the French soldiers were exhausted by their long retreating marches, amidst the heat, the dust and incessant enemy harassment. The Germans reached the Somme on the 28th of August 1914. In the course of this ill-fated series of events, the Battle of Guise – during which General Lanzerac's Fifth Army defied and defeated Von Bülow's troops (28th-30th August 1914) – offered a glimmer of hope.
The German troops were but a few dozen miles from Paris which was not a military target as such.

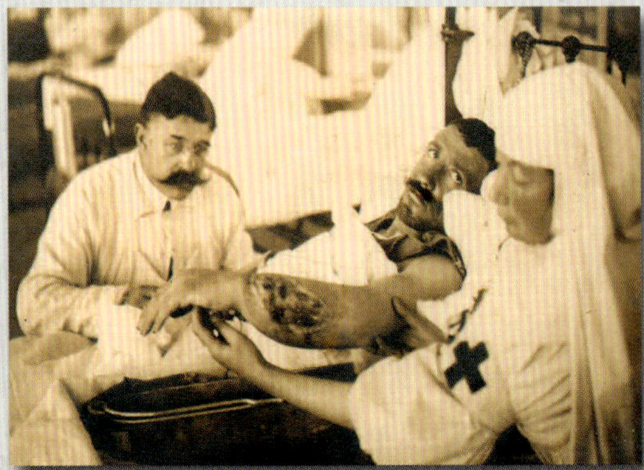

▲ *This wounded soldier's lost gaze reveals the sheer scale of the carnage brought by combat in the year 1914.*

Improvised first aid post set up in a church.

▲ *Temporary graves in the Nieuport dunes.*

From the Battle of the Marne to the stalemate

The German troops were looking to totally annihilate the French army, then to focus their efforts on Paris. A costly error. By making such a manoeuvre, the German First Army, commanded by General Von Kluck (1846-1934), exposed its right flank. Informed of the manoeuvre by airmen who had flown over the German columns, General Joffre (1852-1931) decided to counter-attack. On the 6th of September, he launched a general offensive on a front stretching from the Ourcq to Verdun, commonly referred to as the Battle of the Marne.

From the 6th to the 9th of September, the French soldiers, whose orders were to cease their retreat at all costs, began to attack the German lines. Sealing victory depended on reactivity: reinforcements needed to be despatched as quickly as possible to the different armies. Such was the context that led the Marne taxis to be requisitioned. A total of 600 taxis transported some 6,000 men to reinforce General Manoury's Fifth Army – a role which, although considered as minor, offered them their very own place in the history of the Great War.

With some of its units in difficulty, the entire German combat plan was forced into retreat. It was a slow and progressive withdrawal, which left time for the German Army to organise a solid defensive line upon which the French armies were brought to a standstill from the Aisne to the Meuse.

There was only one way to overthrow the enemy: the race to the sea. From mid-September to mid-November 1914, the German and French armies strove to outflank each other. These deadly endeavours ended in a status quo on the Belgian coast. The front had been "stabilised" over a distance of more than 300 miles. The troops then engaged in a war of positions, more commonly referred to as the war of the trenches. With this perspective in mind, the surge of brotherly spirit on the occasion of Christmas 1914 must be considered as an epiphenomenon within a larger context of ever-increasing brutality.

The first trenches.

Postcard of the 158th Infantry Regiment flag the folds of which symbolise its participation in the Battle of the Marne.

THE ARTILLERY, THE QUEEN OF ALL BATTLES

Artillery was the queen of all battles. Each offensive action was preceded by an artillery barrage aimed at destroying the enemy defences. These bombardments were as destructive as they were devastating for troop morale. In theory, a field artillery regiment was organised in three groups, each group comprising three batteries and each battery being equipped with nine artillery pieces (guns). Each gun was commanded by a sergeant. A battery was, in theory, manned by 3 officers, 15 non-commissioned officers, 156 privates, 169 horses and 22 vehicles. A field artillery regiment was therefore equipped with 81 guns. There were 12 gunners for each artillery piece: 6 servers and 6 drivers.
In France, the French 75cm was the most popular gun, whereas the Germans preferred the 77cm gun. In August 1914, the German artillery had superior firing power and numbers compared to its French counterpart, the latter being forced to make considerable efforts to bridge the gap. Efforts that marked the arrival of more powerful guns: the 155 Schneider and the 155 Rimailho.

▲ *A soldier from an artillery fleet section proudly posing next to a 220mm shell.*

▲ *German artillery piece.*

▲ *Rare snapshot of a heavy gun firing from aboard a barge.*

▲ *Servers using the gun nicknamed "La Panthère".*

▲ *Heavy artillery fire on a railway track.*

▼ *A shell exploding.*

▲ *Imposing 200mm mortar.*

Concurrently, trench artillery and railway guns were developed. The gunner was a technician who adapted his firing based on aerial observations, on information provided by frontline observers and on aerial photography analysis. From inside the trenches, the Poilus had learned to recognise the calibre of a shell from the noise it made as it hurtled through the air. They particularly dreaded shrapnel shells which exploded in the air, releasing 300 lead bullets and causing atrocious wounds.

Background document: Certificate attesting wounds suffered by Brigadier Gouget from the 107th Heavy Artillery Regiment.

'I'M NIBBLING AWAY AT THEM'

Inventing the war: the war of the trenches

At the dawn of the year 1915, the French soldier's appearance was far from appealing. He looked like anything but a soldier. His uniform was old and patched up. To protect himself from the cold, water and mud, he used clothes sent by his family or those collected in almost every town and village throughout France.

Henceforth, he lived in a brand new, horizonless environment: that of the trenches, where life was synonymous to endless monotony. Of course, there were the attacks during which the men had to leave their trenches to try to conquer those of the enemy. But, most of the time, they remained totally idle, in these slumlike shelters where they wrote to their families, played cards, kept watch for hours on end – hours spent struggling, both physically and emotionally to stay as alert as possible.

The front-line trench was at the peak of the defensive system which stretched out over several lines of trenches connected by narrow galleries. There was no question of devising a linear system. The network was a windy, zigzagged arrangement, designed to resist raking from enemy machine guns and fragments of shrapnel.

Between the first enemy trench and the French front line, sometimes only a few feet apart and protected by rudimentary defences (barbed wire networks, etc.),

▲ *Assembling sheep skins to prepare for the winter of 1915-1916.*

◄ *The typical 1915 poilu.*

▲ *Soldiers from the 103rd Infantry Regiment, May 1915.*

▲ *Soldiers from the 34th Territorial Infantry Regiment showing the first gas protection devices issued to troops.*

stretched an area referred to as no man's land, a place where no being dared to live, a place of desolation: full of shell craters, dismembered trees... and bodies. No mistake was to be made: even in times of inactivity, danger was all-pervading; error was not tolerated and proved extremely costly: the cost of life itself.

Death was the common soldier's daily bread. He learned to live with and to anticipate it. Yet, sometimes, that was not enough – in particular when he had no choice but to thrust forward, without cover into no man's land and to face the enemy rifles and machine guns, or when the trench itself fell victim to incessant and violent bombardments.

The trenches were one of the consequences of the superiority of material over men. It marked the era of machine guns and artillery that annihilated any offensive action.

On the 22nd of April 1915, the war became a war of technology, with the use of gas by the Germans in Ypres, heralding the chemical war to come and the ever-increasing use of combat gas. The war needed to be reinvented and that involved calling each and every military strategy into question. In the French Army, there was no time for questioning – the only strategy was attack.

One-off attacks, with no genuine artillery preparation, inevitably deadly and the names of which are engraved in blood: Les Eparges, Vauquois (where Joffre's 'I'm nibbling away at them' took on all its meaning), or large-scale attacks, referred to as penetration, the aim of which was to break through the German lines. In 1915, this type of attack bore two new names: Artois and Champagne.

▼ *Front-line trench held by the 353rd Infantry Regiment.*

The 1915 French offensives

The Artois (9th May 1915) and Champagne (25th September 1915) offensives were the two key penetration attacks led in 1915. Their aim was to break through the enemy front at a specific location, then to exploit this breakthrough in order to sever communication routes and to force enemy retreat and consequent defeat – the domino effect. But, first and foremost, they needed to successfully break through! Both offensives ended in bloody defeats. The Artois attack had served as a "laboratory" for Champagne: the high command learned many a lesson from its bitter defeat and was better prepared for the Champagne attack which began very early, in July 1915, with the rallying of troops in the attack zone – a 22 mile front – and with field preparation (by day and by night) from the front line to a perimeter several miles to the rear.

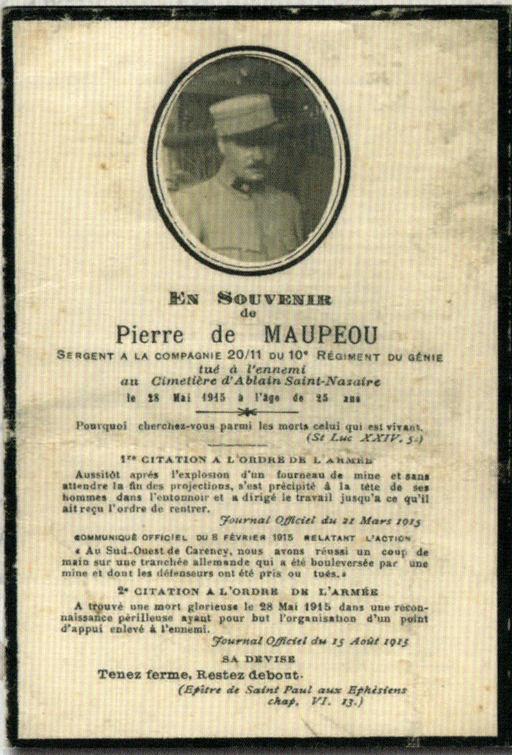

EN SOUVENIR
de
Pierre de MAUPEOU
SERGENT A LA COMPAGNIE 20/11 DU 10e RÉGIMENT DU GÉNIE
tué à l'ennemi
au Cimetière d'Ablain Saint-Nazaire
le 28 Mai 1915 à l'âge de 25 ans

Pourquoi cherchez-vous parmi les morts celui qui est vivant.
(St Luc XXIV. 5.)

1re CITATION A L'ORDRE DE L'ARMÉE

Aussitôt après l'explosion d'un fourneau de mine et sans attendre la fin des projections, s'est précipité à la tête de ses hommes dans l'entonnoir et a dirigé le travail jusqu'à ce qu'il ait reçu l'ordre de rentrer.

Journal Officiel du 21 Mars 1915

COMMUNIQUÉ OFFICIEL DU 8 FÉVRIER 1915 RELATANT L'ACTION

« Au Sud-Ouest de Carency, nous avons réussi un coup de main sur une tranchée allemande qui a été bouleversée par une mine et dont les défenseurs ont été pris ou tués. »

2e CITATION A L'ORDRE DE L'ARMÉE

A trouvé une mort glorieuse le 28 Mai 1915 dans une reconnaissance périlleuse ayant pour but l'organisation d'un point d'appui enlevé à l'ennemi.

Journal Officiel du 15 Août 1915

SA DEVISE

Tenez ferme, Restez debout.
(Epître de Saint Paul aux Ephésiens chap. VI. 13.)

▲ *Memento in memory of Sergeant Pierre de Maupeou from the 10th Engineers Regiments, killed in combat at Ablain-Saint-Nazaire (Pas de Calais) on the 28th of May 1915.*

▲ *German prisoners on their way through the village of Contay (Somme).*

▼ *German soldiers hunting for lice.*

Artillery preparation lasted several days – from the 21st to the 25th of September 1915. Although the defences on the German front line were annihilated, the heavy artillery, entrusted with destroying the 2nd German line along with other targets to the rear, failed to fully accomplish its mission. When the assault was launched on the 25th of September 1915, the troops had just crushed this 2nd German line. The offensive came to a halt on the 6th of October 1915. Leaving an estimated toll of 130,000 dead!

The poilu was no longer the frisky soldier, donning his madder-coloured trousers, that had enlisted in August 1914. He was now a combatant engaged in a modern war, a war of attrition. His appearance had radically changed. Since April 1915, his uniform had taken on the colour that was to make its fame: horizon blue. And since September 1915, the kepi had been replaced with the Adrian helmet. General Joffre had been keen to nibble away at the German Army; however, it was the latter who in fact nibbled away at the French: the year of 1915 was the most deadly of the entire conflict with a total of 349,000 deaths among the French troops.

By the end of 1915, the Poilus were tired and totally incapable of engaging in any further large-scale attack. The idea of a short war was now history.

▲ *A territorial regiment marching in line.*

▲ *Group of soldiers wounded during the Champagne offensive.*

▲ *October 1915 in the Chevalier woods.*

THE TRENCH

Opposing trenches were but a few feet from each other. Through the slits, scouts kept a watch over the enemy trench. Their gazed stretched over no man's land, a neutral and lifeless ground of sheer desolation.

Inside the trenches, the troops tried to kill time. Huddling inside their dugouts, some wrote to their families, others played cards or made rings using aluminium belts from shells. Others, totally dazed by this subterranean life, spent their time sleeping. The familiar sound of the cannonade and the fusillade were a constant reminder that danger was omnipresent and that it could strike wherever, whenever.

Trench periscopes helped keep an eye on the enemy.

View over no man's land.

Inside an officers' dugout.

German soldiers in a trench.

Soldier writing a letter to his family.

▲ *A rear dugout.*

That night, a groupe franc was preparing a coup de main against the German trench aimed at collecting information to report back to the military staff. These feared troops, remained to the rear, waiting for nightfall.

Three days later, they would be relieved. The men would then leave this miserable place by night, amidst the narrow galleries that linked the trenches, to enjoy a moment's well-deserved respite at their camp.

▲ *A French sapper anxiously listening to enemy sap work.*

▲ *A shell has just exploded near a gallery.*

▲ *Machine gun section inside a gallery.*

▲ *View of the battlefield.*

1916

MASSACRES IN THE WEST

The Verdun hell

In France, there is not a single town without a street named "rue de Verdun". Some have even been renamed in honour of the martyred villages of the Battle of Verdun, such as "Allemagne" (Germany), in Calvados, which became Fleury-sur-Orne by council decision in 1916, in honour of Fleury-devant-Douaumont, one of the villages that were destroyed during the extreme combat in the region from the 21st of February to mid December 1916.
On the 21st of February 1916, Lieutenant-Colonel Driant's chasseurs suffered the full thrust of the first phase of the German offensive on Verdun, in the Caures woods. Their desperate resistance at least offered them a place in the legend of the Great War. A wall of steel thrust upon them: the "trommelfever".
The German military staff decided to attack Verdun for two reasons. The first was tactical: to 'bleed to the bone' the French Army. The second was psychological: to capture a site – and its fortresses – that was of symbolic importance in French history.
The Battle of Verdun involved three phases: the German attack (21st February to 4th March), the breakthrough during which the Germans tried to penetrate the front (4th March to 11th July) and the French counter-attack (July to December).

▲ *N°18 personnel transport truck on the Voie Sacrée (Sacred Way).*

◀ *Voie Sacrée conductor.*

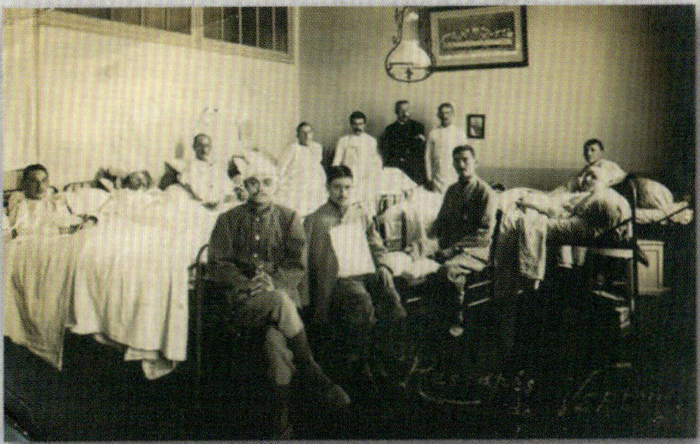

▲ *"The 1916 Verdun survivors".*

It was a battle of symbols, among which the forts of Douaumont and Vaux. Initially lost "without a fight" by the French on the 25th of February 1916, Fort Douaumont was reconquered on the 24th of October 1916. Fort Vaux was lost on the 9th of June 1916. A loss that was nevertheless transformed into victory by French propaganda, by mystifying its defenders' great resistance and by making a national hero of the last pigeon sent by Commander Raynald and his men before the fort surrendered. It was recaptured on the 2nd of November 1916.

Over a battle of equipment: of which artillery was the queen. The trenches were no more; the field was completely overturned by shells, whereas soldiers played a secondary role of simply occupying the terrain.

It was also a battle of men: on the 25th of February 1916, a general was called upon to command operations on the Verdun front. A colossal task awaited him – everything was to be planned and organised, in an extremely short lapse of time. Resistance from the scattered French troops helped thwart the German advances and enabled a fleet of trucks to be brought in to transport men and materials via what was later to be named the Voie Sacrée. His name: Philippe Pétain (1856-1951). On the 9th of April 1916, as the Germans launched their umpteenth attack, he addressed his troops. With his famous, "Courage, on les aura." (Take heart, we'll beat them.)

By mid December 1916, after 10 months of atrocious fighting, the front was "stabilised" on the positions established on the 21st of February 1916. A defeat for the German Army. The Germans had been stopped in their tracks at a cost of 162,000 dead and over 200,000 wounded among French troops, yet the army had not been bled to the bone for German losses were equivalent.

▲ *Soldiers from the 367th Infantry Regiment in the trenches.*

▲ *The Verdun hell.*

A regiment embarking onto trucks on the Voie Sacrée: destination Verdun.

The Somme offensive

Early December 1915, gathered at the French Army's Grand Quartier Général in Chantilly, the Allied army commanders (French and British) decided on a new large-scale operation, the aim of which was to, once more, break through the German front and to weaken the enemy by causing maximum losses. Despite the ongoing Battle of Verdun, that was literally devouring the troops, the offensive was maintained according to plan.

The Battle of the Somme began on the 1st of July 1916. After a week of artillery preparation aimed at annihilating the German positions, the French and British soldiers were confident. But although they fully expected to find not a soul against them, they were faced with fierce German resistance.

The Battle of the Somme was, in a sense, the German soldiers' Verdun, a battle during which they needed to defend every inch of the terrain with one single objective: not to retreat. The result was sheer carnage. Each 11th of November, the British proudly adorn their collars with a poppy, in memory of their youth, cut down in its prime, during this very offensive, in the fields of Somme, a chalky environment where poppies thrive.

Then the rain came, transforming the battle into total chaos. Losses (killed, lost or wounded), for the sole month of December 1916, were of 498,000 British, 440,000 French and 414,000 German soldiers.

Late 1916, the opposing camps found themselves in the same situation – both Verdun for the Germans and the Somme for the French and British were failures. In both cases, minimum ground had been gained against maximum losses. It was the year of massacres in the West. Furthermore, a certain weariness had taken over the ranks as they faced this deadly and interminable war.

▲ *German prisoners after the Battle of the Somme.*

A British infantry regiment heading for the Somme.

▲ *French prisoners after the Battle of the Somme.*

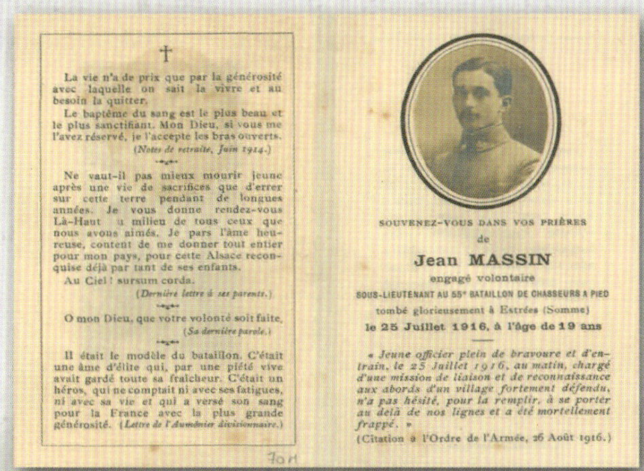

†

La vie n'a de prix que par la générosité avec laquelle on sait la vivre et au besoin la quitter.

Le baptême du sang est le plus beau et le plus sanctifiant. Mon Dieu, si vous me l'avez réservé, je l'accepte les bras ouverts.

(Notes de retraite, Juin 1914.)

Ne vaut-il pas mieux mourir jeune après une vie de sacrifices que d'errer sur cette terre pendant de longues années. Je vous donne rendez-vous Là-Haut au milieu de tous ceux que nous avons aimés. Je pars l'âme heureuse, content de me donner tout entier pour mon pays, pour cette Alsace reconquise déjà par tant de ses enfants.

Au Ciel ! sursum corda.

(Dernière lettre à ses parents.)

O mon Dieu, que votre volonté soit faite.

(Sa dernière parole.)

Il était le modèle du bataillon. C'était une âme d'élite qui, par une piété vive avait gardé toute sa fraîcheur. C'était un héros, qui ne comptait ni avec ses fatigues, ni avec sa vie et qui a versé son sang pour la France avec la plus grande générosité. *(Lettre de l'Aumônier divisionnaire.)*

70 M

SOUVENEZ-VOUS DANS VOS PRIÈRES

de

Jean MASSIN

engagé volontaire

SOUS-LIEUTENANT AU 55e BATAILLON DE CHASSEURS A PIED

tombé glorieusement à Estrées (Somme)

le 25 Juillet 1916, à l'âge de 19 ans

« Jeune officier plein de bravoure et d'entrain, le 25 Juillet 1916, au matin, chargé d'une mission de liaison et de reconnaissance aux abords d'un village fortement défendu, n'a pas hésité, pour la remplir, à se porter au delà de nos lignes et a été mortellement frappé. »

(Citation à l'Ordre de l'Armée, 26 Août 1916.)

▲ *Memento in honour of Second Lieutenant Jean Massin from the 55th Chasseurs Battalion, killed at Estrées (Somme) on the 25th of July 1916.*

▲ *A nurse from the 23rd Infantry Division in the trenches.*

◀ *Liaison officers from the 226th Infantry Regiment in the Somme (August 1916).*

LETTERS FROM THE POILUS

On the front, the soldiers were totally isolated from the outside world, their only link being correspondence. As from August 1914, interactive exchange of letters between soldiers and their families began. For the combatants, these letters were a genuine supplement to their physical nourishment. Reading offered them an opportunity to think themselves back with their loved ones and to take part, by proxy, in their day-to-day family lives (for example bringing up children or looking after the farm).
The military authorities had fully grasped the importance of mail for maintaining troop morale. As soon as general mobilisation was launched, a military mail service was initiated.

▲ *The Dillingen (Germany) POW camp parcel service.*

Soldier from the 31st Infantry Regiment reading a letter (1915).

Prior to November 1914, a letter sent to a combatant on the front went through six different steps: from the sender to the regimental depot, from the depot to the army collection station, from the station to the border office, from the border office to the paymaster's office, from the paymaster's office to the mail delivery officer, and finally from the mail delivery officer to the addressee. A complex organisation that was quick to reach its own limits given the great volume of letters and parcels.
In December 1914, the distribution channel was alleviated via the 'creation', or rather the reorganisation, of the Bureau Central Militaire (central military bureau), established at the Conservatoire National de Musique de Paris (today the Paris Conservatory), which, henceforth, centralised all letters and parcels before forwarding them to paymaster/distribution offices, referred to as the secteur postal (postal

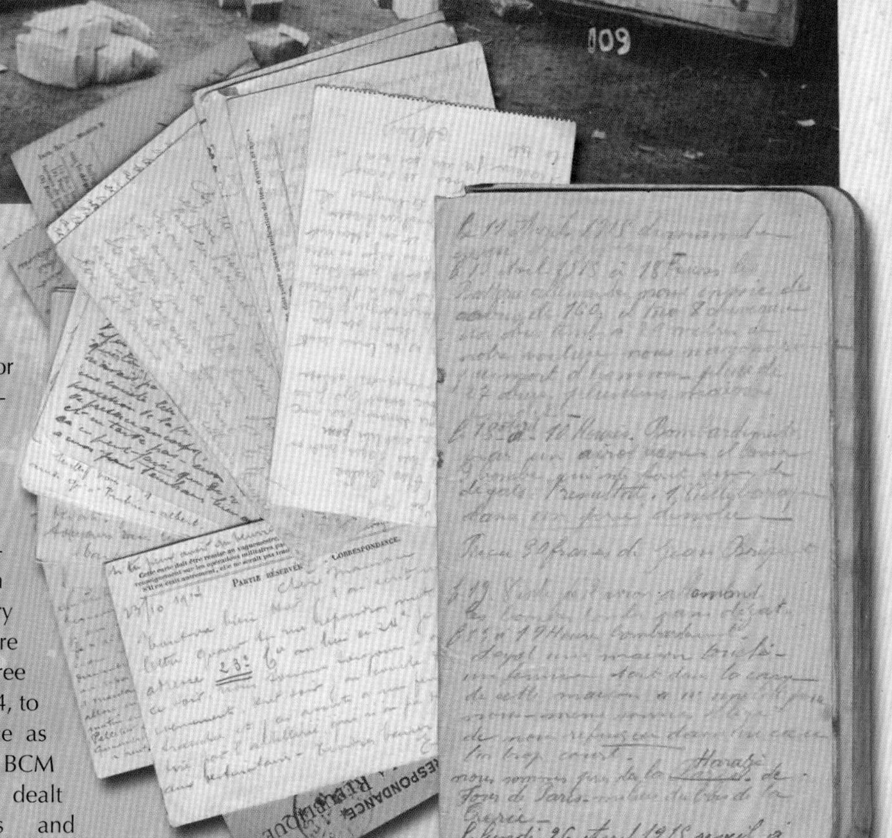

▲ *Mail delivery officer from the 318th Infantry Regiment sorting mail by appropriate company.*

sector). Each postal sector was given a number corresponding to a postal district comprised of military units.
For example,postal sector 167 dealt with correspondence for units from the 10th Colonial Infantry Division. These sectors were created following a decree dated 11th December 1914, to genuinely come into force as from January 1915. The BCM (central military bureau) dealt with 3,500,000 letters and 150,000 parcels every day.

◀ *A postal section vehicle.*

Soldiers confided in their diaries – a way of keeping a trace of what they never thought they would see and of evacuating their daily horror through prose. ▲

1917

In a gallery near Braye-en-Laonnois (Aisne), in June 1917.

FROM THE CHEMIN DES DAMES OFFENSIVE TO THE MALMAISON VICTORY

Farewell to life... Farewell to love

Despite the disappointments of 1915 and 1916, the French Army generals hung onto the idea of putting an end to the conflict (by provoking the fall of Germany) via a violent attack preceded by artillery preparation that would break through the enemy lines. One high-ranking French officer, General Nivelle (1856-1924), had already earned himself an excellent reputation. He had replaced General Pétain at Verdun in May 1916, commanding the French counter-attacks from July to December 1916. He was behind the highly symbolic recovery of Forts Douaumont and Vaux. Then in December 1916, he replaced General Joffre in command of the French armies.

The collapse of Russia to the East was of concern to the military staff for the Germans could now repatriate troops to the Western Front. The decision therefore needed to be made before they arrived. General Nivelle had a plan. He hoped to launch a surprise attack at a specific location on the front with prior artillery preparation that did not exceed 48 hours. Despite great scepticism among other generals, including Pétain, the offensive was maintained. General Nivelle was totally blinded – he had no doubt as to the success of his plan – for was he not the great victor of Verdun? Yet, there were many clear signs that should have aroused doubts: the main one being the strategic withdrawal devised by the German Army on previously prepared defensive positions – a sign that all German forces were aware of his plan.

▲ *Dallon bridge at Saint-Quentin, destroyed by the Germans as they retreated in April 1917.*

The Chemin des Dames offensive was launched on the 16th of April 1917. Prior bombing had no impact on the German defences. As soon as the artillery barrage came to a halt, the German soldiers came out of their concrete shelters – "creûtes" (cavities hollowed out in the sandstone rocks) – and fired on the French waves of assault, resulting in sheer carnage. The attack was brought to a permanent halt on the 19th of May 1917. From the 16th of April to the 19th of May, the French army lost over 140,000 men (killed, lost or wounded).
General Nivelle, who was later named the "bourreau" (the executioner) by the Poilus, was replaced as commander-in-chief of the French armies by General Pétain on the 15th of May 1917.
The French soldiers had had their lot of continuous slaughter. Across the entire front, at greater or lesser degrees, groups of soldiers refused to return to combat. This was not a matter of refusing to do their duty – of deserting – but simply an expression of their discontent with regard to these repeated offensives that were as deadly as they were futile. Their demands essentially concerned improving their living conditions: food, leave, etc.
Today, when ordinary citizens discuss the Great War, the subject of the 1917 mutinies inevitably crops up.

▲ *Front-line kitchen on wheels.*

In November 1998 during a visit to Craonne (one of the key offensive sites around the Chemin des Dames), the French Prime Minister Lionel Jospin requested that the mutineers be reintegrated within the "national collective memory". His initiative immediately spurred unwarranted controversy over their rehabilitation – an aspect the Prime Minister had failed to anticipate. Proof that the subject is highly sensitive in France. A review of the number of "mutineer" soldiers executed needed to be conducted and the resulting total, according to the Defence Historical Service, was 55.

▼ *The Restaurant des Permissionnaires with the canteen women in the foreground.*

▼ *Squad from the 135th Infantry Regiment in 1917.*

As in 1916, General Pétain found himself in a critical situation; sanctions were as necessary as was a certain degree of flexibility. Sanctions involved bringing leaders before a council of war to be judged. Flexibility was in the form of improved living conditions for the Poilus, including better supplies and, in particular, more frequent leave.

General Pétain restored order and became highly popular among the Poilus. The 1917 year end offered France two victories thanks to painstakingly prepared operations, in Verdun in August and in Malmaison on the 23rd of October, the latter implying the use of planes and combat tanks which proved decisive for victory and essential for limiting human losses.

This year end was also synonymous to painfully lacking numbers for the French Army as it found itself in a defensive position on the Western Front. The German staff had its western positions reinforced with divisions which were no longer useful in the East following the Russian collapse. All they could do was to hang on in there and wait for the "Sammies": Pétain's famous, "I'm waiting for the tanks and the Americans".

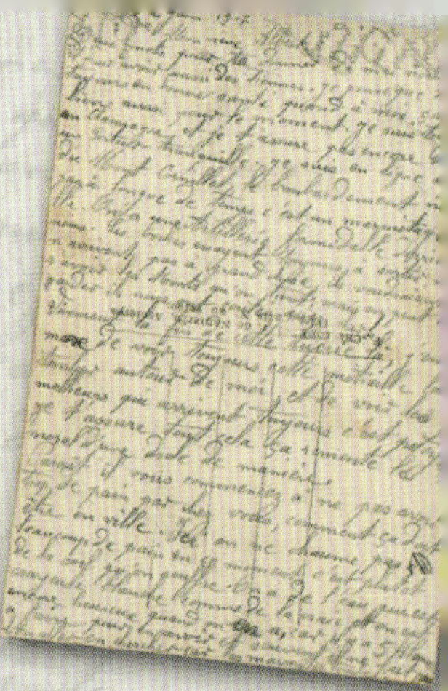

2nd of June 1917
My dear friend Albert,

Just a few words to send you some news and to ask for yours in return. I suppose that you are still in good health, as for me, all is well for the time being. I am still posted in Champagne and, I can assure you, not yet in the quietest of sectors. I am in the Mont Cornillet lines and with the incessant bombing comes terrible heavy shell. We have fantastic artillery behind us. The Boches keep trying to get out but never make much ground, they'd like to get back the hills we're holding onto, but we can keep them, they've cost us enough!

Here's hoping the end of all this killing is near, I've had my lot of seeing more and more grapeshot fall all around me, and of seeing misfortune happen all the time, it's pitiful. I can tell you, it all gets your spirits up in the strangest way. We're told you're starting to have trouble finding bread at home, what must it be like in town. Here, we're not too short of bread right now, we suffer more from thirst. We have chalky white water and, even then, we're happy to have it, for we have to go 3 miles to get it and it's not always a great idea because the heavy shell keeps falling;
From your great chum who fondly shakes your hand.
George

▼ *November 1917 in Champagne.*

Before the Malmaison attack

Lafayette, we're here!

On the 6th of April 1917, the United States declared war on the Triple Alliance, hence breaking a long tradition of neutrality. It did so despite the pacifism of its President, Woodrow Wilson, for its trade (in particular based on sales to nations within the Entente) was threatened by the excessive submarine war led by the Germans since February 1917. The reason put forward for the United States' entry into the war was the torpedo attacks on American ships by German submarines. On the 7th of May 1915, the cruise liner Lusitania was torpedoed and 124 American citizens were killed. The attack provoked great shock in the United States - shock that was to be used in 1917 by American propaganda to urge soldiers to enlist.

An early contingent of "Sammies" arrived at Saint-Nazaire on the 26th of June 1917, but larger numbers of US troops only landed in France much later. In the meantime, French instructors were sent to the United States to train future combatants.

American soldiers

1918

THE ULTIMATE OFFENSIVES

The swan song

Soldiers from the 144th Infantry Division with their gas masks..

For the Germans, there was only one alternative – to attack before American reinforcements could arrive. To do so, General Ludendorff (1865-1937), commander-in-chief of the German armies, was provided with divisions that had been repatriated from the Eastern Front. Hence, what was referred to as the "Imperial attack" began on the 21st of March 1918. The Germans innovated technically by using, behind the mobile artillery barrage, small groups of highly mobile combatants that could intervene on a need-be basis: "Strumtruppen". The war of movement was back in force but it was of no resemblance to the one in August 1914, for it counted far more on material than on men.

From March to July 1918, the Germans attacked in all directions. They even came within 40 miles of Paris. The Allied front was weakened throughout, but it did not break. However genuine the German victories, they could not be fully exploited due to exhausted troops and lack of reinforcements. In contrast, the Allied armies could count on the reinforcements that were so lacking on the German front. Furthermore, since the 26th of March, they had a unique commander: General Ferdinand Foch (1851-1929).

The Americans entered the scene, much to the admiration of the Poilus as they resisted the German advance and, in particular, as they captured the Belleau woods, which became the symbol of their engagement in the Great War. From the 30th of May to the 5th of July 1918, to conquer these woods, the American suffered losses of 8,100 men (killed, lost or wounded).

▲ *Soldiers from the 114th Infantry Regiment's 10th company who survived the 26th of March 1918.*

Allied counter-offensives and armistice

The last German offensive took place on the 15th of July 1918. It was totally futile: the Allies had been informed of its date by prisoners. After taking the precaution to evacuate the front lines, hence rendering the German artillery barrage ineffective, the Allies drove back the enemy offensive and counter-attacked on the 18th of July 1918 in the Marne.
For the German Army, it was the "beginning of the end", the 8th of August 1918 being considered by historians as its day of bereavement. The German front was broken in several places and the Germans retreated. On the 12th of September 1918, the Americans progressed towards Saint-Mihiel (Meuse). On the 26th of September, the Allies launched a further attack. To the bitter end, the German retreat was methodical, and deadly for both sides.

▲ *11th November 1918: the joy spurred by the end of the war was shadowed by the pain of having lost a loved one during the conflict.*

◀ *Souvenir picture of the day of the armistice for these non-commissioned officers from the 202th Field Artillery Regiment's 29th Battery.*

On the 7th of November 1918, a German delegation approached the French lines. With an aim: to discuss peace conditions.
Discussions which, at the 11th hour on the 11th day of the 11th month – the 11th of November 1918 - sealed the end of combat on the Western Front. The Germans signed the armistice in a train carriage in Rethondes (Oise), in the Compiègne forest. As France celebrated the end of hostilities, the end of four years of war, all around, widows and orphans cried for their loved one. One of the 1,383,000 French soldiers who would never return home.

An American soldier casually watching two French soldiers firing from their anti-aircraft machine-gun position.

Controversial peace

It was an armistice, not a surrender. During the peace conference that was held from the 18th of January to the 6th of May 1919 in Versailles, the Allies had great difficulty in agreeing on the sanctions to be applied to Germany and its allies; the Americans took the lead. Finally, on the 28th of June 1919, it was in the Hall of Mirrors in the Palace of Versailles, a highly symbolic site for it was precisely the place where the German Empire had been proclaimed in 1871, that peace was signed... yet it already bore the seeds of World War II.

Germany suffered severe sanctions: it was to pay for the extensive damage caused by the war, it lost its colonies, conscription was forbidden and its territory was reduced by one eighth. The Germans referred to the treaty as a "Diktat".

A new map of Europe was in the making. A map that lacked both coherence and consideration for ethnic disparities.

▲ *The "carnet de la victoire" victory booklet was issued to soldiers. They could use it to note their campaigns, their wounds and their service record. It was like a Great War road book.*

▼ *22nd November 1918: souvenir picture of the Great War for these officers from the medical service.*

The 1st section of the 28th Infantry Regiment on the front on the 1st of January 1918.

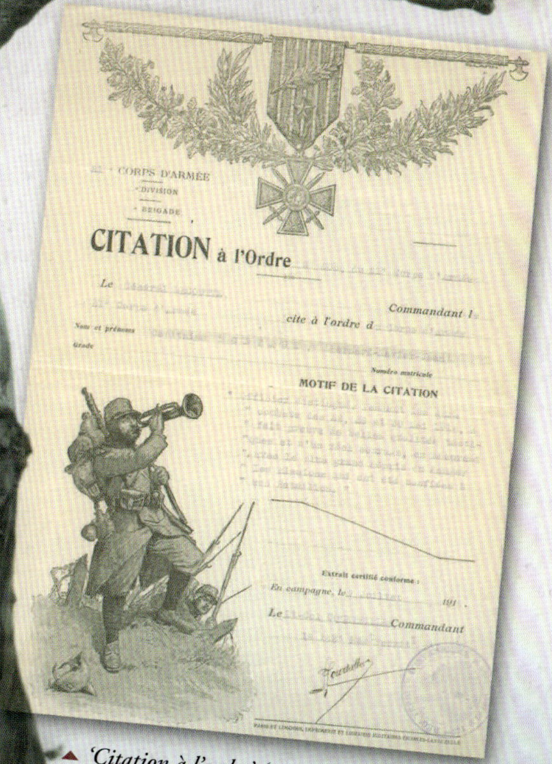

CORPS D'ARMÉE
DIVISION
BRIGADE

CITATION à l'Ordre

Le

Commandant

cite à l'ordre d

Nom et prénoms

Grade

Numéro matricule

MOTIF DE LA CITATION

Extrait certifié conforme :

En campagne, le 191

Le Commandant

'Citation à l'ordre' (military commendation) awarded to Captain Montaut's 21st Corps – 143rd Field Infantry Regiment.

The face of Marianne, mutilated by a shell in 1944, on the Trévières (Calvados) war memorial, is a constant reminder of the false hope around what was supposed to be the War to end all wars.

THE TOLL

Terrible human losses for France

They include 1,383,000 soldiers lost from a total of 8,410,000 mobilised troops (i.e. 900 killed every day). 18.9% of all officers and 16.1% of troops had been killed on the 1st of June 1919.

The most severely affected age class (a man born in 1892 was in the 1912 class) was that of 1914, with 85,200 dead from a total of 292,000 enlisted, i.e. 29,2% of all combatants in the group.
The number of wounded is estimated at 3,594,900 including 15,000 gueules cassées , 100,000 mutilated or amputated and 42,000 blind or one-eyed.
Among the wounded, 60% had been hit by shrapnel, 34% by bullets and 0.3% by knife.
Material losses were more difficult to assess. A few figures:
4,500km2 of forest were destroyed,
21,000km2 of farm land ravaged,
800,000 houses ruined.

A "gueule cassée".

Ruins.

Horses, the innocent victims of the war.

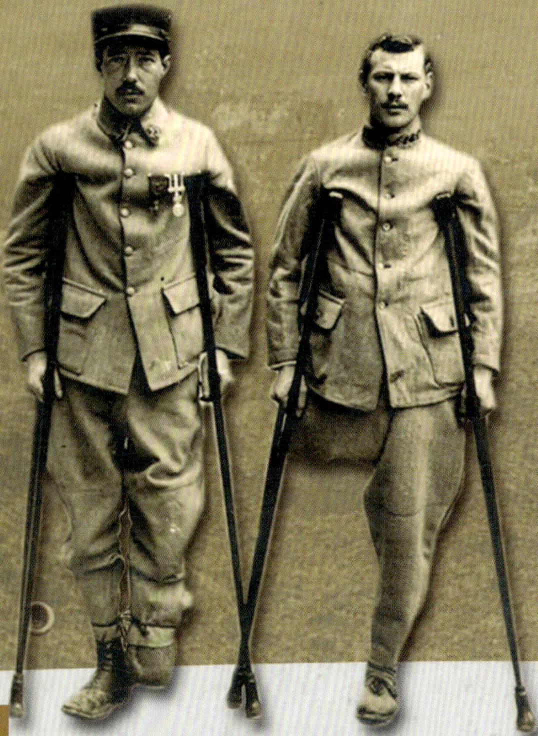

War cripples.

A nation of "killed in action".

▲ There is a war memorial in honour of war victims in almost every French town and village. Most often patriotic, it can also be pacifistic. It is generally located in front of the town hall or the church.

▲ Gunners from the 254th Field Artillery Regiment posing with a young girl from Alsace. Alsace-Lorraine had been reconquered, but for how long and at what cost?

▸ War cripple.

Background photo: The combat zone was devastated, the land no longer fit for farming.

SOURCES

A few sources for those who like to delve into historical documents

Looking up the past of one of your forefathers who took part in the Great War is a relatively simple affair. All you need is a date and place of birth. Indeed, this information alone paves the way inside local archives where you can consult the regimental record pertaining to your family member. Let's take an example: your great grandfather was born on the 7th of July 1887 in Caen. Then all you need to do is to head for the Calvados archive department and consult the regimental record for Mister X, born on the 7th of July 1887 in Caen, class 1907 (simply add 20 years to the date of birth), recruited in Caen. You will then be able to consult an A3 format register comprising a succession of regimental records for all soldiers from class 1907, each record including the following information: civil status, particulars, education level, change of residence, service record, wounds and commendations. Thanks to the service record, you will discover the regiment(s) in which the person fought. With this information, you can then consult the Journal des Marches et des Opérations – JMO (war diary) for the regiment in question at the Service historique de la Défense (Defence Historical Service) in Vincennes. The JMO enables you to retrace the person's movements during the Great War, on a day-by-day basis. You will also be able to associate photographs taken during the conflict, and your documents (letters, military passbook) with the official story of his regiment.
Should an annotation on the regimental record indicate that the person was wounded, all you need to do is to write to the army hospital and medical archives to gain access to the person's medical file.
If the person was an officer, his file can be found at the Service historique de la Défense in Vincennes and you can identify the file number in the officers' registers at the scientific desk in the reading room.
If your ancestor was killed in combat, you will find step-by-step instructions for your research in another book from the same collection: "Mort pour la France".

◄ *JMO for the 79th Field Artillery Regiment, classification mark 26N790, which you can consult at the Service historique de la Défense-Terre.*

▲ *The information in the regimental record and consultation of the JMO will enable you to date your photographs.*

▲ *If your ancestor was killed during the war, then the first thing to do is to consult the "Mémoire des Hommes" website.*

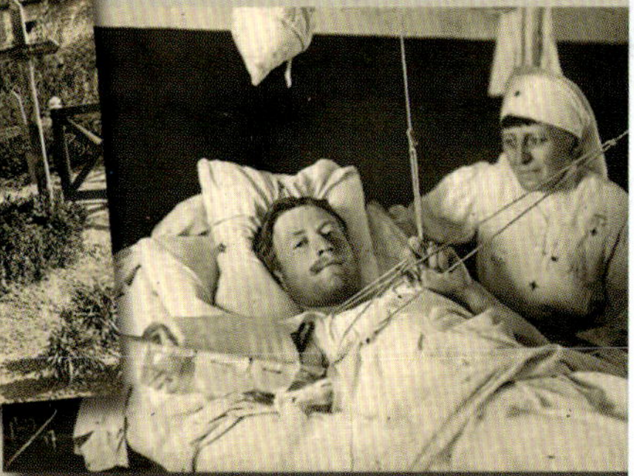

▲ *If your ancestor was wounded, once you have consulted his regimental record, write to the army hospital-medical archives for information on his wounds and his hospital admission.*

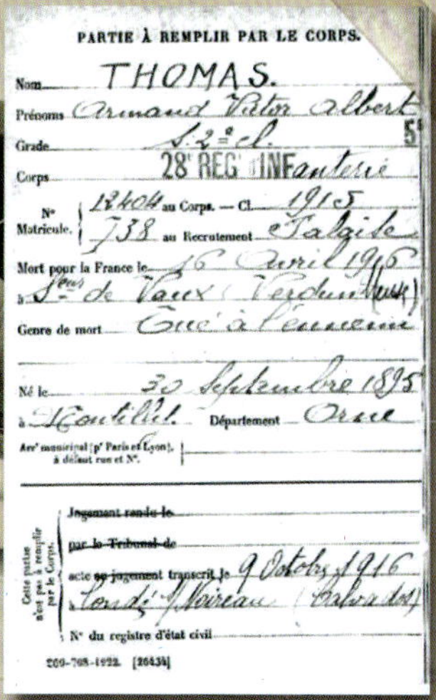

PARTIE À REMPLIR PAR LE CORPS.

Nom THOMAS.
Prénoms Armand Victor Albert
Grade S. 2e cl.
Corps 28e REGt INFanterie
N° Matricule. 12404 au Corps. — Cl. 1915
738 au Recrutement Falaise
Mort pour la France le 16 Avril 1916
à Bois de Vaux (Verdun Meuse)
Genre de mort Tué à l'ennemi
Né le 30 Septembre 1895
à Montilly Département Orne
Arr. municipal (p^r Paris et Lyon), à défaut rue et N°.
Cette partie n'est pas à remplir par le Corps.
~~Jugement rendu le~~
par le ~~Tribunal de~~
acte ~~ou jugement~~ transcrit le 9 Octobre 1916
à Condé s/ Noireau (Calvados)
N° du registre d'état civil
209-708-1922. [26434]

▲ *Example of a "Mémoire des Hommes" record.*

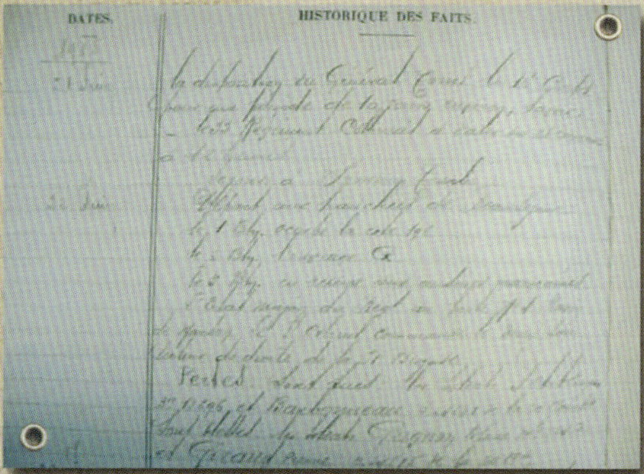

▲ *Excerpt from the JMO for the 33rd Colonial Infantry Regiment. A day-by-day history of the regiment.*

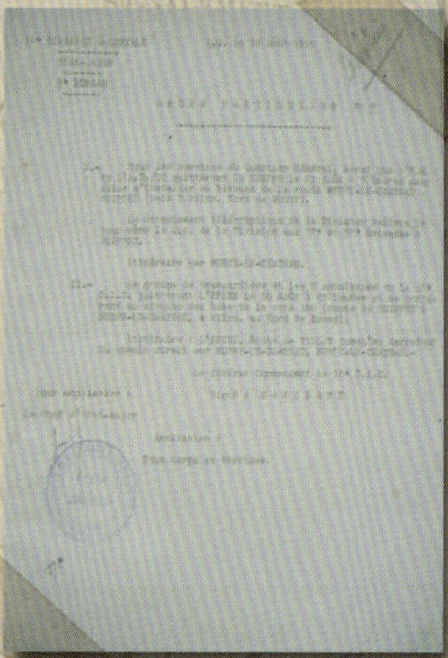

▲ *If you want to take your research even further, then don't hesitate to delve into the archives for the brigade, division or army corps. They include operation reports, detailed maps, etc.*

Almost all regimental records can be consulted via local archive websites. The "Mémoire des hommes" website enables you to consult the JMO for each unit, the war dead register for France, the register of executions and that of military aeronautical personnel.

CONCLUSION

This chronology, when studied concurrently to photographs of the Poilus, offers a new perspective for understanding the living conditions of French soldiers in all theatres of operation on the Western Front. Once replaced within their context, all presented photographs take on a particular dimension and enable us almost to join the poilus in their trenches, and to imagine their moral and physical suffering. They take us well beyond simple chronological landmarks, giving a face to each and every one of the 1,357,800 French soldiers that were killed during the conflict, during what was hoped to be the "War to end all wars".

They fully contribute towards the historiographical debate which confronts two schools: that of constraint and that of consent. These schools strive to explain why and how these soldiers managed to endure four years in the trenches. According to some, the soldiers had no choice - they were obliged by the political and military authority. For others, those in favour of the notion of consent, it was a question of doing one's duty for one's fatherland, of defending the national soil, qualifying war as a crusade.

Yet beyond these debates, there are stories, individual stories that emerge. For who has never heard of a family ancestor lost during the war? Of another, who survived the hell, who coughed and spluttered every time he spread fertilizer over his fields because of exposure to combat gas? These stories are precisely what the enclosed chronology has striven to bring back to life.